# WHAT MY BODY NEEDS TO GROW! A KID'S FIRST BOOK ALL ABOUT NUTRITION

## Healthy Eating for Kids

Children's Diet & Nutrition Books

**PRODIGYWIZARD**
BOOKS

Our body is made of billions of cells. Each cell is designed to perform certain functions. Cells have to be well-nourished so they can do their jobs, and so your whole body can work well.

In order to live and work, your cells need water, oxygen and nutrients. These include carbohydrates, proteins, fats, vitamins and minerals.

These vitamins and minerals are carried by the blood cells to the rest of our cells. Where do these vitamins and minerals come from?

# Oxygen

We badly need this in order to live. It comes from the air that we breathe.

As we breathe in, oxygen passes into the lungs and goes into the blood. Millions of red blood cells are contained in every drop of blood.

These carry molecules of oxygen to the cells in our body. The best way to fill up the body with oxygen is by taking deep, slow breaths of clean air.

# CARBOHYDRATES

Grains like wheat or rice and beans are good sources of carbohydrates. These are broken down into sugars. Our brain runs on sugar.

So we need
carbohydrates-rich
foods like potatoes, rice,
fruits and vegetables.

Complex sugars are
absorbed by our body
and can give us energy
over a long time.

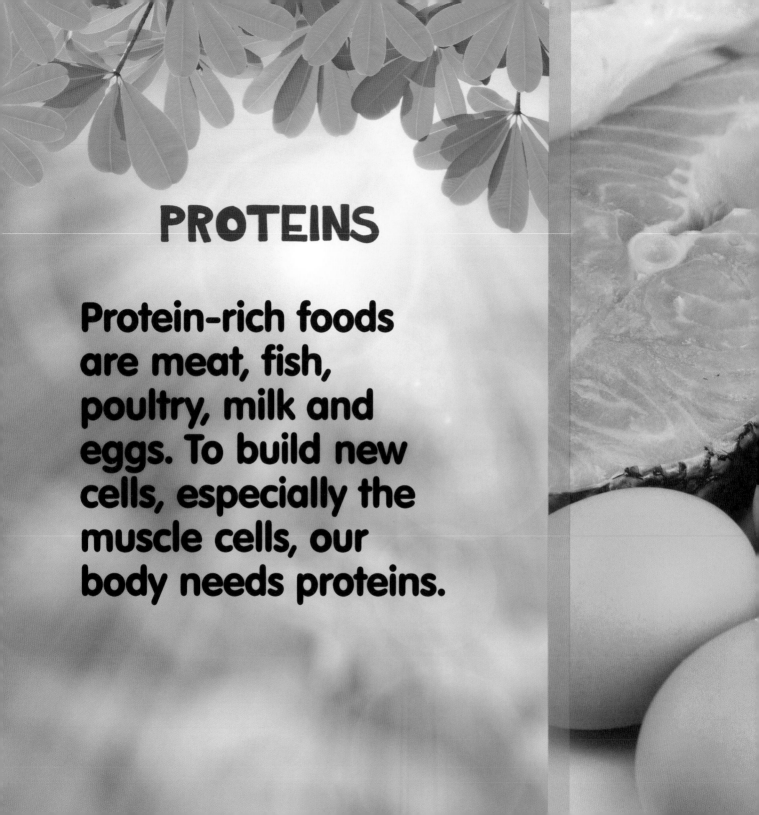

# PROTEINS

Protein-rich foods are meat, fish, poultry, milk and eggs. To build new cells, especially the muscle cells, our body needs proteins.

# GOOD FATS

To keep our internal organs warm, our body needs a certain amount of fat.

This is also to provide us energy when we exercise. Fat-rich foods are nuts, avocados, olives, milk, cheese and some types of fish. But, as with all the things we need, avoid eating too much fat. If you eat more than the body needs, it does not help you.

# VITAMINS AND MINERALS

These are found in most healthy foods. Fruits and vegetables are known to be rich in vitamins and minerals.

Although our body needs only a small amount of these, they don't stay long so we have to eat foods with vitamins and minerals every day.

# CALCIUM

It maximizes bone growth and is the most abundant mineral in the body. For a normal heat beat, a small but significant amount of calcium is in the blood stream.

# FIBER

For good nutrition and healthy growth, our body needs fiber. Fiber fends off constipation especially among children. High-fiber foods are whole grains, legumes, fruits and vegetables.

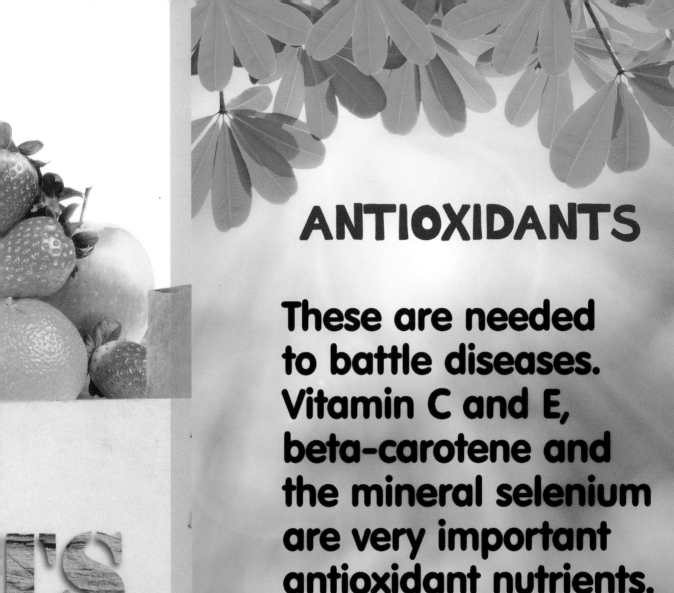

# ANTIOXIDANTS

**These are needed to battle diseases. Vitamin C and E, beta-carotene and the mineral selenium are very important antioxidant nutrients.**

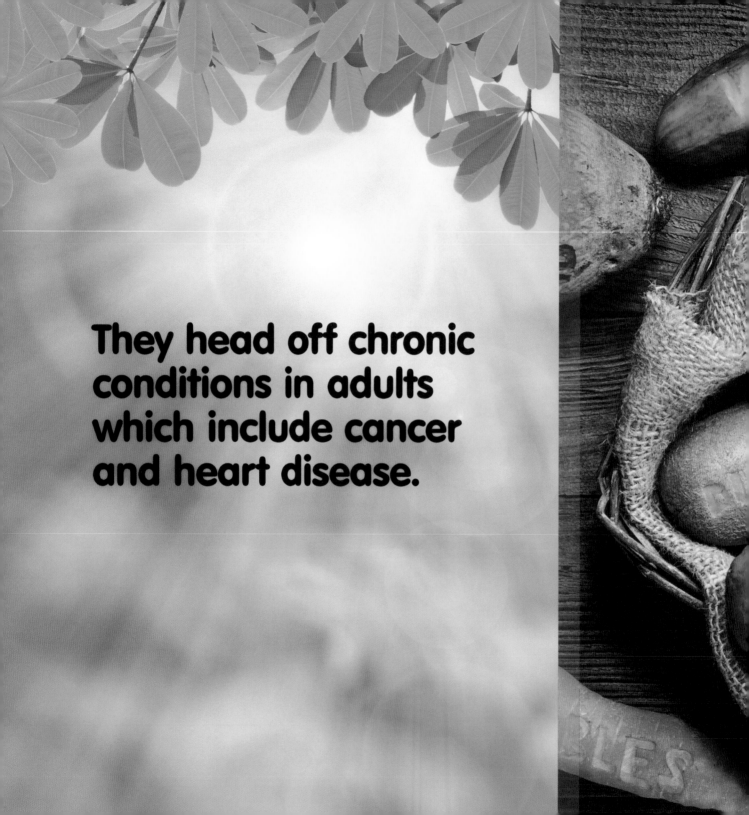

They head off chronic conditions in adults which include cancer and heart disease.

According to experts, antioxidants are the superheroes of nutrients. They battle free radicals that are products of air pollution, cigarette smoke and strong sunlight.

Antioxidants-rich foods include berries, broccoli, spinach, sweet potatoes, and carrots.

# IRON

It is another essential nutrient that our body needs in order to grow. Our bodies must have enough iron to grow with. The red blood cells need iron. This is to transport oxygen to every cell in the body.

Iron also has an important role for brain development and function. Iron deficiency is most common among infants, children and pregnant women.

Animal products like meat, sea foods, and the dark meat of poultry provide the body with heme iron, which our blood and muscles need.

We have to eat nutrient-rich fruits and vegetables. They provide us with fiber, potassium, Vitamin C, magnesium and folate (including folic acid).

They are also good sources of Vitamin A. We all need these for essential growth.

No one specific food or food groups help you grow better than others. We need a well-balanced diet in order to grow in a healthy way.

**We need enough calories, carbohydrates, proteins, fats and essential vitamins and minerals. We need these for normal growth.**

Made in the USA
Lexington, KY
25 October 2016